pain,
love,
& purpose

CHRISTINA RICE

Published and distributed by Golden Hour Publishing.
Rice, Christina
Pain, Love & Purpose
ISBNs
978-1-959513-00-1 Paperback
978-1-959513-01-8 Hardcover
978-1-959513-02-5 eBook

dedication

to everyone who taught me how deeply i can feel.
thank you for being my muse.

contents

about the book

this book of poetry is about the moments, people, emotions, and stories that make us who we are. this book is about how pain leads us to purpose, and how we can turn our mess into our message. it's a story of heartbreak, grief, doubt, fear, insecurity, and sadness. it's also a story of love, passion, exploration, curiosity, growth, evolution, transformation, and purpose. it's a story about growing up, finding yourself, and loving yourself. it's a story about the power of emotion. it's the story of my heart's journey.

preface

writing this poetry book was an accident. the last time i wrote poetry was probably in high school for an assignment in literature class, and i'm sure the poem was nothing to write home about. i've always loved to write, but it felt more natural for me to express myself through prose than through poetry. if you're wondering how i accidentally wrote a poetry book, i am still surprised by it myself. here's the story.

it started on a gloomy saturday morning. i rolled out of bed and went downstairs to whip up a latte and curl up on the couch with my journal, prepared to process far too many thoughts that had been nagging at me for weeks. an extremely busy period of my life had overlapped with an intensely transformational one, as i found myself moving through yet another cycle of death and rebirth. i felt completely unraveled on every level and needed space to find inner clarity. it was the first saturday in months that i had nothing to do, so i planned to stay in my pajamas and journal it out for a few hours, or for as long as i needed.

fuzzy blanket, binaural beats, candles lit, mood set—in a peaceful setting, i was ready to let my thoughts flow. what started out as automatic writing quickly snowballed into something else. i heard a loud voice in my head that sounded like my own, but far more ethereal, and as if i were speaking through a microphone. as i heard the words, my hand flew across the page of my journal, and it was as if that voice and my heart merged into one. the words were like a river current that couldn't be stopped. what came through was a poem describing a painful memory. in writing it, i reconnected with the emotion from that time, and i felt it move through. after the energy had space to rise to the surface, it was like the memory could finally come to a close.

after that poem, another came through, and then another. a stream of poems continued for three days straight until it finally stopped. complete. each poem detailed a specific memory, relationship, or emotion that was ready to be alchemized. as i wrote, i laughed, i cried, and i healed. each of these stories needed some space to breathe, to be felt, to be read, and to be heard. the expression came through the lens of the version of me in that moment, at that time. i have a different perspective on many of these memories now, but the version of me who lived the story wanted some room to say her piece. in alchemizing each of those moments, i felt a shift, a release, an ending, and a beginning. these poems are a tribute to that version of me—the one who lived these experiences and emotions.

there's something quite beautiful about exploring both the simplicity and the complexity of individual moments in our lives— the ones that make us who we are. the "big" moments certainly shape us, but it's actually the collection of "smaller" moments that has had the greatest impact on who i am and how i see the world. in simple moments, there can be so much complexity. what has truly shaped me have been the people i've met and the moments i've shared with them—friends, lovers, family, and strangers have all been my teachers and impacted me in profound ways. in writing these poems, i realized the specific moments and relationships that my subconscious decided were most significant in shaping me up to this point. some of those moments caught me by surprise, but they brought me clarity. in simplifying the complex emotions and relationships in my life, i found my alchemy.

i've been obsessed with understanding purpose since i was a child— asking a lot of big questions at a young age and not receiving many satisfactory answers. when you feel emotions so intensely, for both yourself and others, you have to wonder what the purpose of the pain really is. as i got older, i started to explore the idea that maybe pain itself could be the path to purpose. not that we need to experience pain to feel purpose, but if we do experience it, how can we transmute it instead of letting it hold us back? holding onto the grief, fear, or pain, from big events or small moments in life, only hurts us more. we can choose to transform those energies. feeling really is the path to healing.

pain is relative and comes in so many forms—emotional, physical, mental, spiritual. from stubbing your toe, to getting your heart broken, to grieving a loved one, to sickness, to betrayal, to abandonment, to abuse. both "big T" and "little t" traumas impact us and deserve space to be processed and alchemized so we can find the wisdom from the pain and use that to help us move forward from an empowered place. some of the deepest pain and fears we store in our bodies might be from simple moments that our adult brains try to dismiss, but we can't underestimate how much getting teased on the playground or having one rude comment thrown our way might impact our nervous systems in the long run. it all matters.

the nature of life is movement, change, and transformation, and pain can be a powerful catalyst for that. pain cracks us open to the point of surrender so we can see the things we couldn't before. through surrender, we open our hearts to experiencing real, deep love in all its forms. if our hearts are closed as a protection mechanism, how can we really feel love? it's love that heals us and guides us. it's love that shows us our purpose—not as a destination, but as a way of being. i've seen again and again in my life how my pain has led to my purpose, and how the things that break us also build us. in writing each of these poems, i found even more purpose within each moment of pain, love, loss, and transition. if articulating an emotion i've experienced helps one person feel a bit more understood and a bit less alone, then it's served a bigger purpose.

stories are my favorite way to learn and better understand myself. it's through the stories of others that i uncover emotions and inner truths that i might not have recognized before. it's through the stories of others that i feel seen and less alone. even if we don't go through the exact same experiences, our emotions connect us to each other. i spent so much of my life feeling alone, even though i wasn't, and wondering if i would ever feel truly understood. underneath that was a craving for real, deep love. underneath that was actually a craving to truly know and understand myself.

writing this healed me, and i hope it brings you some healing, too. if nothing else, i hope these poems remind you that you're not alone. i truly believe that every moment of pain, no matter how big or small, can be alchemized and help pave the path for us to experience deeper, truer love. and when we experience that, we remember our purpose.

pain

disclaimer

writing is how i process
it's how i learned to feel
i find some words to help explain
emotions that are real

if you don't like what i say
or how i really feel
then maybe simply go away
or find a way to deal

when you don't like my words
i wonder if you know
you were inspiration
but now you're welcome to go

the other side

people think nothing shakes me
but they don't know the truth

they don't see me cry at night
mental breakdowns in my room

they don't know the pain i've felt
that cuts through me like a knife

they don't know the fear i have
when i anticipate the fight

what they see is strength
and what they see is true

but there's a side of me
they haven't seen
and she deserves love too

frozen

i never will forget
that dreary, gloomy day
we walked out of a funeral
with nothing else to say

not one, but two lives lost
they were both so young
i wanted to go home
i felt completely numb

as we walked back in our classrooms
the teachers locked the doors
something else was happening
my heart dropped to the floor

do we hide under the desks?
the teachers closed the blinds
they told us to be quiet
as they turned off all the lights

i wished i had my phone
to send my family a text
i didn't want to think about
what might happen next

they told us not to worry
the SWAT team was near
i could hear the sound of helicopters
buzzing in my ears

i felt my body stuck in freeze
i was far past numb
when i went to school that day
did not anticipate a gun

all there was to do
was sit quietly and wait
that was catholic school
but the first real time i prayed

i told myself that soon
this would all be over
imagined going home from school
and crying on mom's shoulder

and finally they told us
it was safe to make a sound
but the tension in my body
never felt unwound

that's a day at school
i'll never quite forget
a memory imprinted
the problem not solved yet

take back your box

i feel your expectations
so much pressure put on me
you wish i'm someone different
please just let me be

you pushed me in a corner
you put me in a box
and then you want to punish me
for someone i am not

i say no to your expectations
and to who you want me to be
i will not accept your projections
a reflection of you, not me

i ripped open your box and stepped out of it
ran away as far as i could
you yelled and you screamed as i did the things
you said i never would

you can take back your box and stand in your corner
and spew hate at the light that you see
but i created the life that i wanted
from your fear, found who i could be

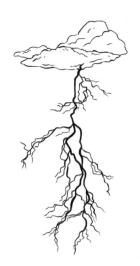

heartless

the screams, the fights
the tears, the lies
you chose to ignore
my deafening cries

i wanted you to see my pain
thought maybe then you'd stop
but when you saw me at my weakest
it went from bad to over the top

after that i changed direction
shut up like you wanted me to
i hardened and hid in my shell
now you say you never knew

innocence

the memories are blurry
every weekend felt the same
we went to different places
but same dynamics, different names

we said that we were having fun
and i think that we believed it
but as we lost control
the only option was to see it

we thought if we were numb
we could finally let go
feel something, make connections
and access the unknown

at first it was fun and games
until it got too real
until we got ourselves in danger
and we weren't equipped to deal

and at that point we realized
we weren't quite yet adults
suddenly we craved innocence
and the love we needed most

truck lights

i waited for the lights
looking for your truck
because the nights when i was scared
you always picked me up

and we would drive somewhere
that felt far enough away
and lie there in the truck bed
where i was safe to feel the pain

we looked up at the stars
there wasn't much to say
in an empty parking lot
we found our getaway

the tears streamed down my face
and i could hardly breathe
you held me close and stroked my hair
and let me simply be

that was my safe space
where i let myself release
the feelings kept inside
with you i found my peace

but then there came the time
when you had to drive me back
you dropped me off with the reminder
that strength i did not lack

the blame game

you ask me to be generous
but then you cut me off
you want to take, and take, and take
and then refuse to talk

you like to have someone to blame
to point at someone else
but now i see the games you play
and i'll remove myself

then you get upset with me
but you still don't want to talk
you prefer to judge and blame
if that's your choice, i'll walk

if you want to make up stories
at least have the decency
to include me in the conversation
if your stories involve me

but you don't want to do that
you know exactly what i'll say
if you had to own up to your lies
you wouldn't last a day

sticks and stones

sticks and stones can break my bones
but words can never hurt me
really? 'cause words can fucking hurt
pretending otherwise won't serve me

they say actions speak louder than words
but words are pretty loud too
it's what you mean that i can feel
in what you say and what you do

accountability and forgiveness
can we learn to balance those out?
admitting that words can hurt us
and giving the benefit of the doubt

there's a fine line between strength
and bypassing your emotions
keep pretending you're fine when you're not
and one day you'll start to feel frozen

for a long time i thought i was strong
when really i was just numb
numbness might dull the pain
but it also blocks the love

so i learned to admit i was hurt
to express the things i used to hide
and when i stopped judging emotions
i found my real strength inside

caught

i told you that you hurt me
tears welled up in your eyes
i called you out directly for
your deception and your lies

you thought you'd go behind my back
and i would never know
do you even know me?
don't bother with the show

the blunt conversation
took you by surprise
you didn't think this meeting
would make you want to cry

i need accountability
if you want us to be friends
and if you won't own up to it
then this will be the end

remember when i told you
i'd never get upset
at anything you said or did
but lies i can't forget

and if you just apologize,
own up to it—we're good
but if you hide behind excuses
i'll end it like i said i would

unforgivable

in a painful moment, you threw words
that were daggers to my heart
i didn't know you had it in you
to rip our relationship apart

i called it unforgivable
no going back from there
i never looked at you the same
a memory i could hardly bear

they say that time can heal all wounds
but i'm not sure that's true
perhaps with time we can gain
perspective that is new

those daggers in my heart
stayed there for quite some time
it hurt too much to pull them out
so i pretended i was fine

but those daggers made me tired
i went from red to blue
keeping them inside, i gave
my power away to you

so i decided to forgive you
i slowly pulled them out
i bled some more in agony
and then i made a vow

to release anger and resentment
for me, not for you
but i noticed as i healed for me
there was some healing for you too

blackout

it was late on friday afternoon
when i finally woke up
head pounding, body aching
i didn't bother getting up

i tried to recall anything
that happened the night before
my roommate stumbled in
someone else knocked on the door

the night was very blurry
flashes popped up in my mind
as it got pieced together
i was happy i survived

that blackout was the worst
it was my final straw
after it i had the thought
i didn't know myself at all

i wondered how i got there
it wasn't even fun
and i laid there in frustration
who had i become?

i became the person
i said i never would
and i did the things
i thought i never could

and i knew it wasn't healthy
to drink my pain away
but i had never learned quite how
to deal another way

disappointment in myself
embarrassment for sure
i had lots of motivation
and stopping was the cure

so overnight i stopped
decided to be sober
honestly i don't regret
my party days are over

fallen hero

i put you on a pedestal
my hero every time
but then i watched you crumble
it shattered me inside

you did your best to handle
the cards that you were dealt
but i could never understand
the type of pain you felt

i did my best to support
the choices that you made
but when they started hurting me
respect started to fade

and then you threw away
the little that was left
drowning in your pain
i couldn't watch what happened next

it's not that i don't love you
i always will, i know
but i love myself enough to leave
when nothing more can grow

central park

you were always smiling
you made everybody laugh
people felt the joy you brought
in every photograph

we had inside jokes
that bonded us at first
you were the type to always
cheer your friends up at their worst

most people did not know
the other side of you
they only saw the guy who laughed
made jokes, lit up the room

over time, we lost touch
but then i got a call
i got the news in central park
was not prepared at all

no one saw it coming
that you'd end your life so soon
our hearts all broke in unison
as we mourned the loss of you

and in the years that followed
reminders of you came
i felt your presence all the time
just in a different way

sometimes i reminisce
look at old photos of us
and it makes me think a lot about
how time is not enough

i hope you know the impact
you had on every life you touched
and even as years pass
we all miss you very much

tit for tat

where did you all go?
overnight they left
at my darkest moment
looked around at emptiness

i guess i thought you'd have my back
after those years that i had yours
but maybe that's too much to ask
to expect my values to be yours

i didn't think it was too much
to ask you just to listen
but you called me a burden
i'm not sure that's yet forgiven

you made your own meaning about
what it meant when i asked you for help
i didn't want you to take it on
just needed a safe space to melt

now we're on the other side
and you come back around
you want me to be strong for you
can i take that on right now?

i start to see that sometimes
people have to go through it themselves
to learn to have compassion
for when others are not well

and so i get to choose
how i show up this time
should i be the bigger person?
it's easy to decide

i choose to be who i needed
when i felt like everyone left
i'd rather write a new story
than recreate when i was depressed

and so it is forgiven
because holding on is pain
and i can understand that
with new examples, we can change

amnesia

locked myself inside the room
you're yelling through the door
slurring insults that will trigger me
we've been here before

i sit there and i take the hits
you don't mean what you say
that doesn't mean it doesn't sting
too late to run away

tears are streaming down my face
how much longer can you scream?
you're blacked out, have no control
the punching bag is me

the worst part is you won't remember
anything you said
tomorrow or next time i see you
that's the time i dread

because you act like nothing happened
do you really not remember?
or are you just pretending?
admit it? you would never

you switch personalities
which one will i get?
daytime you are kind and gentle
nighttime you're a threat

i tell myself it's not really you
it's just the alcohol
but deep down i hate to say
i don't believe myself at all

narcissist

i really tried to love you
i tried so hard it hurt
but the longer that i stayed
everything got worse

lines were blurry—was it love?
or enabling your behavior?
in the end i crumbled
i couldn't be your savior

you told me to feel guilty
that all the fault was mine
that i caused all your problems
without me, you were fine

and at first i took it on
blamed myself for all the pain
until one day i recognized
all the games you played

narcissists are sneaky
they'll get inside your head
manipulated me for years
brainwashed by what you said

it took me getting far away
to wake up from hypnosis
still weaving your big web of lies
stuck in your psychosis

i think what scares me most is
you believe the lies you tell
too comfortable with fallacies
the truth would hurt like hell

and no one stands a chance
in setting those lies straight
to your stories you're committed
any challengers you hate

most people are afraid of you
scared to get caught in your web
one wrong move—you'll take them down
make up things they never said

but since i've made it known to you
that i see and know the truth
now you're the one who's scared of me
the tables turned on you

should've known

i gave you a second chance
an opportunity to grow
i was ready to truly forgive
to start over from what i know

at first i thought you could do it
thought you could change and be a true friend
but once again i was fooled
there was betrayal and then an end

thought we had a stronger foundation
a sense of mutual respect
but i guess it was silly for me to think
i could forgive and forget

so now i've learned my lesson
don't set expectations too high
i often fall for potential
now i don't really know why

how did we get here?

i often wonder how we got here
how we let it get this far
but one thing led to another
now we realize where we are

and sometimes it seems hard
to find the right way out
you think ignorance is easier
than finding strength to turn around

but ownership is admirable
accountability—the way through
we have to look at what didn't work
or we're not really starting new

so there's the choice—acknowledgment
or pretending it's not there
from your response i start to see
the truth of if you care

ten people

the worst night of my life
lying on the floor
we had a nasty fight
and i could take no more

i collapsed where i was standing
and crawled into my room
i cried until i thought my bones
might break, this pain was new

i had hit my limit
after what you said
in that moment i really thought
that i'd rather be dead

that was my darkest moment
and i did something sick
i told myself i'd call ten people
if no one answered, that was it

and so i got to five
and no one had picked up
i was heaving, barely breathing
an awful way to test my luck

i'd had the same dark thought
many times before
but this time it was different
i meant it in my core

and that was what was scary
the moment was right there
had a plan, quick and easy
i thought no one would care

i stared up at the ceiling
to really think it out
i realized that if i gave up
they win, and have an out

to be honest in that moment
i changed my mind because
i wanted to prove them wrong
for them to pay for what they'd done

and then i felt so guilty
because those were my thoughts
and i screamed out loud to god
asked him to show me what he wants

and then my cell phone rang
as i was lying on my back
seven people in
and the third one called me back

so i took that as a sign
to get back on my feet
to ask for help but recognize
no one else would fight for me

and from that heavy night
i uncovered my real need
wanted someone else to save me
that's my responsibility

so i made myself a promise
to show up and succeed
to not wait around for someone else
to prove they cared for me

that's when my life changed
that's when i took control
i chose to heal and love myself
to listen to my soul

coffee shop

for a few months no one talked to me
in loneliness i drowned
when i needed someone most
felt like no one was around

so i went to different coffee shops
for a change of scenery
with other people all around
felt a little less lonely

but i also hated going out
because people often stared
it was that or stay stuck in my room
i had no energy to care

one day at the coffee shop
i was immersed in a new book
a woman sat down at the countertop
and i could feel her look

i was used to people looking
but this look wasn't the same
it felt more curious than anything
she walked up and asked my name

she didn't want to overstep
but she'd regret not reaching out
she didn't know what i was going through
but could she help somehow?

she didn't want to make assumptions
but she saw herself in me
a few years back she deeply struggled
at the time she looked like me

she slipped me a folded paper
with a number i could call
she said, "if you need someone to talk to
don't hesitate at all"

her assumptions were incorrect
but her kindness left me stunned
i wanted someone to understand
never thought a stranger would be the one

it wasn't that i was invisible
people just didn't know what to say
i realized i had abandoned myself
that stranger changed my life that day

the whole story

awhile ago, there was a phase of my life
i tried to forget, push away
i refer to it as the dark ages
deep in darkness, everything changed

things had built up for awhile but
dramatic shifts came overnight
one trigger—my body spiraled
and i was called up to the fight

it started as lots of strange symptoms
and then my organs shut down
desperately trying to find the root cause
as my weight fell to 70 pounds

i was terrified and confused
it was something i couldn't control
i felt hopeless, needed answers
too much to deal with at twenty years old

some doctors said i was lying
and others kept running tests
others said i was shit out of luck
they could only take their best guess

i dropped out of school and i hated myself
who was i without achievement?
an identity built around intellect
shattered, i couldn't believe it

i couldn't keep my words straight
forgot the sentence i said before
a struggle to hold conversation
didn't know what to do anymore

i brought a hefty binder with me
that tracked every symptom and update
with labs and tests, a collection of notes
the doctors could not keep it straight

of course with so many specialists
things are bound to get missed
like giving me meds for opposite problems
the whole time i felt dismissed

as my body shut down a bit more each day
i truly could not believe
that someone could give a prognosis so morbid
without any empathy

i grew weaker each day, it got harder to breathe
had to stop and sit down on the stairs
the migraines, the brain fog, the aches, and the pains
discomfort was too much to bear

i hated when people would hug me
i felt like my body might break
i wouldn't let anyone touch me
sympathetic mode—stuck wide awake

random lump on my throat, swollen ankles
is that my blood in the sink?
i asked all my doctors, what's happening?
but still no answers for me

i got so used to the physical pain
over time i just couldn't care
the worst part was being trapped in my head
i had to admit i was scared

i was a regular at the hospital
getting new bloodwork each week
when i looked in the mirror i didn't recognize
the person that they said was me

people often stared at me
they always gave me that look
when they made comments, let it roll off my back
all of my strength that took

but i was getting mixed signals
one day an intervention
the next an agent asks me to model
lots of unwanted attention

a man sends food to my table
tells me that i need to eat
my boss asks what diet i'm on
and what's my workout routine?

meanwhile my doctors are fighting
some want to send me away
i feel like a child, it's out of my hands
they don't ask me if i am okay

if i have to take one more supplement
i think that i might choke
if another rude comment gets thrown my way
i'll collapse from insensitive jokes

my days became lots of bloodwork
clinical trials and pills
a medical mystery—their best advice
was "take some time off to chill"

most of my friends fell silent
until one day i found out
conversation was loud behind my back
spreading false rumors around

judgment from every direction
i didn't need it from anyone else
uninformed people had plenty to say
too tired to stand up for myself

they made lots of assumptions
that they never said to my face
but they were happy to make up those rumors
i decided to set the facts straight

i wrote an article telling my story
a few things i needed to say
the story took off, overnight it was featured
on the front of the national page

abandoned, rejected, and judged
that's how i felt deep down
i worked so hard to be little miss perfect
now forced to stop and slow down

being perfect wouldn't save me
control freak at my core
and doing everything "right" didn't fix it
who was i really living for?

i was forced to surrender
and change the way that i lived
and in burning my identity
a new life could begin

i got into meditation
boundaries became my friend
i started to do shadow work
gave my heart a chance to mend

i reconnected with my soul
and healed my inner child
and in rewiring my brain
found parts of me i exiled

so i got to know myself
the real me—not the fake
i made a promise i would live for me
a commitment i was glad to make

my life path took a turn
my magic came online
and through the twisted road i found
who was always on my side

through my loneliness and pain
searching in the dark
i found out who i really was
from her i'll never part

if it hadn't all come crashing down
would i have ever made choices for me?
the universe broke down my ego
and through it, set my soul free

stirring the pot

this is the thing about people
they hear it the way that they want
even if you communicate clearly
they'll still twist it to something it's not

if someone is truly committed
to a story, a lens, a belief
they'll always find a clever way
to distort what you really mean

that says more about them than you
and i wonder, what is that like?
to be so unhappy that you look for ways
to make others wrong so you're right

this is the thing about people
they find the evidence they want
to confirm whatever they already think
and then they keep stirring the pot

backstabbed

for you i gave my all
poured in everything i had
and on the other side
i never thought i'd get backstabbed

when i had to leave
it was truly for myself
from your jealousy and anger
you painted me as someone else

you really didn't like it when
i chose my health instead of you
in giving everything i had
i lost myself to you

you shut off conversation
no chance to talk it out
you said i was the villain
no objections were allowed

it definitely scares me
how loyalty is rare
you pretended to be on my side
then changed your mind without a care

you used to mean so much to me
i clung to memories we made
but in the end you flipped a switch
i was left feeling betrayed

what i can see

for a very long time i thought
you really just didn't like me
but recently i discovered
you've been scared of what i can see

you're scared that i might out you
because i see through all your lies
you like to hide behind your masks
with me you can't even try

and so if you don't like the truth
you probably won't like me
i have no interest in your illusions
i'll be honest about what i can see

trust issues

i have a habit of opening up
to people who just want to take
i'm not sure why that's who i choose
unneeded problems i make

but now i've decided to change that
to practice discernment with who
i open my heart to and who i let in
it's easier to say than to do

in trying to end my self-sabotage
i saw how it did serve me
when i opened my heart to those people
i stayed some version of free

free from getting my heart broken
that's what happens when you let someone in
free from emotions i cannot control
i'm scared that's a game i can't win

free from attachment to others
a valid reason to get out
i created my own trust issues
but i think i figured it out

i know who the right people are
they'll meet me where i'm at
but i can't keep on expecting
betrayal, rejection, attack

when i open my heart to someone
with the capacity to see me
now i'll have to really feel
they'll love me or they'll leave me

then the risk of abandonment
likes to pop into my mind
but the chance at love and real connection
is worth it every time

lost in translation

it's obvious to me
things got lost in translation
it would really help if we
improved communication

i'm trying to be clear
that i want us to be friends
but instead of listening
you create more stories in your head

if you would simply talk to me
we could clear the air
all i ask is for some time
so i can truly share

misunderstandings happen
when people aren't direct
i'd love to be direct with you
but you haven't let me yet

you can keep creating stories
or you can just find out
how it is i really feel
if you agree to talk it out

the old you

there's pushing and there's pulling
i'm tired from the drama
i don't have time for twisted games
you blame it on your trauma

you say that it can work
but i can't count on things to change
you say that you are different
after all your time away

maybe in some ways you are
in places deep inside
but when we talk, it's the old
you i recognize

so i let you go because i know
someone else is better for you
and then you kick and scream and prove
my suspicions were quite true

rumors

you keep on coming back
like a leech i cannot shake
you suck the life right out of me
my light you try to take

you try to shake my confidence
you keep on spreading rumors
i'm shocked at who you became
and that i didn't see it sooner

but it wasn't who you became
rather who you really are
you told me you had changed
but clearly you were wrong

fool me once, shame on you
twice—i should've known
i guess that's on me to not
expect that you had grown

i have a habit of giving people
the benefit of the doubt
and then it bites me, knocks me down
will i learn my lesson now?

but i refuse to let you
take my trust away
that there are loving people
whose loyalty won't sway

you keep on spreading rumors
and it makes me wonder why
you spend so much time and energy
on someone you don't like

through you i've learned a lot about
what i will allow
in my life with open arms
my standards higher now

and so i'd like to thank you
for helping me to see
those rumors are a compliment
not everyone's for me

shattered

somehow i got caught up in you
i lost myself in us
i gave it everything i could
but my best was not enough

after you i wondered
who i really was
could i really trust myself?
i thought you were the one

i tried to pick myself back up
glass shattered on the floor
i was broken into pieces
couldn't handle any more

how could i forgive myself?
how could i be so blind?
for awhile i was sure
now i think i lost my mind

the hardest part about it was
trusting me again
but piece by piece, glued back together
i found the strength to stand

the pain that built me
(here i am again)

heart pounding in my ears
blurry vision took my eyes
legs turned to lead
i'm stuck in bed
am i running out of time?

shivers up and down my spine
stuck in panic mode
aching body
cracking joints
i'm trapped in this alone

in and out of fever
nausea if i see a screen
just to lift one finger
takes all my energy

i thought of all my friends my age
living much simpler lives
i never thought i'd be so young
fighting to survive

the anger came in many waves
i screamed up at the sky
i would try anything
tears welled up in my eyes

my stomach getting ripped to shreds
i think my skull might burst
i hear screeching in my ears
pray it will not get worse

imprisoned in my body
fatigue was all i knew
all i could feel were aches and pains
numb from emotions too

the thing is from the outside
i looked like i was fine
they can't see the pain i'm in
i'm torn up deep inside

so they would ask for one more thing
and i thought i might break
it took every ounce of energy
to give a smile that was fake

i hated them seeing me struggle
over years i got good at pretending
put on a brave face, don't let them worry
because pity would be never-ending

everyone asks how i'm feeling
the question i hated the most
because every day i felt the same
getting better—i never felt close

for a decade i fought for my health
lived life as the girl who was sick
my sadness and anger found no direction
there was no one to blame for this

my life was quite different from people my age
but i healed and then i could see
although i once thought that pain stole my life
that same pain is what truly built me

suffocated

you tell me to be quiet
you tell me to fit in
you tell me not to rock the boat
only safe place is within

i can't believe you live that way
always choosing out of fear
i'm not supposed to say too much
don't worry—you were clear

who knew my thoughts were so threatening?
sounds like the problem is yours
it's because you can't handle a different opinion
that your self-oppression endures

poison

you take pride in judgment
in passing clever, rude remarks
i wonder if you care that you
inject pain with every dart

it took me far too long to see it
the insecurity inside
the ways you made me question me
and trust more in all your lies

thanks for the dart you shot my way
it instantly woke me up
and i knew i had to walk away
couldn't leave you fast enough

you still take pride in judgment
makes you feel better than the rest
i know deep down it triggers you
that without you i'm at my best

snowball

i don't really know what to tell you
when you complain about problems you make
if you don't like it then why don't you change it?
you're the common factor at play

you can use your energy to complain
or you can use it to make something new
you can decide to do something different
no one can take that power from you

but you keep choosing the same old things
i wonder what it is you expect
you want someone else to fix it
paralyzed in pursuit of respect

you're so afraid to get anything wrong
that you never make any moves
you're so concerned about what they think
you feel you have something to prove

the more that you overthink it
the more problems you start to create
snowballing, wrong direction
caught up in the sacrifice made

at some point you'll have to come to a stop
if you want to switch directions
but you'll have to choose something other than
a sense of false protection

is it really easier
to stay exactly where you are?
seems more painful to stay unhappy
already let it get this far

just because you're used to it
doesn't mean it's comfortable for you
if you can create your problems
you can surely solve them too

time bomb

he called me a time bomb
i said, what the fuck?
i'll take that as a sign
it's time that we break up

i'm a liability
because i have emotions
because i speak my truth
it causes way too much commotion

he said i'm too okay with change
he likes stability
but that's why he stays stuck
sounds like a boring life to me

i think he's the time bomb
one day he'll just blow up
from all those trapped emotions
i'll be gone when he combusts

on my own

you share your opinion that
i'm throwing everything away
but the way i see it
that's what will happen if i stay

it bothers you i trust myself
to jump into the unknown
i'm confident in what i'll achieve
when i'm on my own

you never had that confidence
and you don't trust yourself
i won't take on your projections
send those to someone else

open wound

i had never felt so vulnerable
i had never felt so raw
i was being honest
and you told me i was wrong

with you i walked on eggshells
but then i heard them crack
when i realized how i really felt
there was no going back

the only way was honesty
to share fully how i felt
and so i told you everything
you blamed someone else

you told me that my feelings
weren't a good enough reason
you said i was overreacting
and it was just the season

i couldn't believe the audacity
to say my feelings weren't enough
to blame it on the time of year
and that "this patch was rough"

and so it was my moment
to really speak my truth
and i had the realization
i suppressed myself with you

but it was time to change
i stood firm in my position
you refused to walk away
for a month we felt the friction

i felt like i was drowning
the wounds stayed raw and open
you kept instigating fights
nothing left unspoken

it honestly felt really good
to let all my feelings out
to finally express to you
my frustrations and my doubts

it's sad to me it took the end
for you to finally see
all the times you didn't listen
or take me seriously

it felt like pulling teeth
cutting all the cords
but after that i found my healing
the wound is raw no more

lost

after it was over
i wondered who i was
i felt that i had lost myself
it frightened me because

i spent so much time devoted
to understanding me
but in that deep reflection
i still couldn't fully see

misunderstood

sometimes i think no matter what
no one will ever really get me
i feel the subtle disconnect
i pretend it doesn't upset me

can anybody understand
what's underneath my words?
how i feel and what i think
and how i see the world?

is anybody listening?
my cries fall on deaf ears
i think no matter what i say
no one will ever really hear

they try, but they don't get it
that's the disconnect i feel
i know someday i'll find it—
a connection that is real

transition

when you left, the world fell silent
held my breath for far too long
i didn't have the space to feel
for others i stayed strong

when you left i couldn't cry
i coped by going numb
i was blocked from feeling pain
also blocked from feeling love

i coped by staying busy
so feelings can't catch up
always looking forward
one day i had enough

i was driving on a sunny day
windows down, i felt the breeze
your song came on the radio
the one you always sang to me

my unhealed wounds were triggered
i pulled over, let it out
as i wept over my steering wheel
my heart started to shout

things i didn't want to hear
feelings i didn't want to face
my bloodshot eyes said it all
my grief needed some space

so i let myself feel broken
and i took some time for me
my heart had time to mend
you helped me find my peace

i see you in the butterflies
that sit on flowers at the park
i see you in the stars at night
that twinkle when it's dark

i see you in red roses
that grow in my backyard
and in hummingbirds that fly by
you never feel that far

now i see loss quite differently
"transition" is what i prefer
and even though it's different now
in ways you feel much closer

i used to think i needed time
but how much is enough?
you taught me you can never lose
somebody that you love

boundaries

bitchy with my boundaries
that's what some might say
but i will tell you what it costs
to give my peace away

everybody tugs on me
it comes from all directions
a favor here, a question there
my heart needs more protection

far too many access points
and messages every day
over time it all adds up
i'm pulled in every way

then i reached my breaking point
and one day i realized
in being there for everyone
i left myself behind

so i crawled into my hole
admit i can't keep up
my body's breaking down on me
she tells me that's enough

i often feel like i'm
a completely empty cup
zero gas left in the tank
that's when they always call me up

it's always in those moments
when no energy is left
i have nothing else to give
that's when i get more messages

just one small quick favor
and just one tiny question
it all adds up and all my time
is spent in your direction

i try to find the balance
but the truth is i can't be
the one who's there for everyone
the forgotten one is me

it's not that i don't want to
show up for you it's just
there are far too many people
who pull on me at once

when i tried to please everyone
i betrayed myself
my body broke when i neglected
me for everyone else

i'm sorry

i'm sorry for the times i didn't listen
i'm sorry i didn't hear your cries
i'm sorry for not paying better attention
and the years i didn't realize

you were guiding me all along
in ways i did not understand
i was so stubborn that i couldn't see
you reaching out for my hand

i overlooked your wisdom
i didn't trust your love
disconnected from my inner voice
no scream was loud enough

so i kept pushing and forcing
trying to do it my way
and if i had stopped, i could've heard
your cries for more rest and more play

and eventually we crumbled
i was pushed to full surrender
i felt the darkness overwhelm me
a time it hurts me to remember

brought to my knees and humbled
i couldn't force my way out
had to face what i was avoiding
had to admit my fears and my doubts

i had lost all trust in you
but it was never your fault
i was the one who made the choice
to bring our healing to a halt

because i wouldn't listen
because i wouldn't feel
the pain, the hurt, the fear, the sadness
but that was the way to heal

so i'm sorry i didn't listen
and i promise i will now
i've learned you're always on my side
healing comes when i allow

rainbow

i lived my life in color
neon, bright, and bold
rainbow was my brand
no plans to fit the mold

an expression of my energy
vibrancy and joy
the entire world my playground
colors were my toys

as i got older, things got darker
and i felt quite depressed
so i started wearing black
to represent the heaviness

that black gave me protection
it was my way to hide
tortured in my sickness
i kept everything inside

no longer felt like neon
i was bruised in black and blue
hiding in my cave
i was safe to see my wounds

through that space of darkness
i slowly found the light
and it was time to cleanse myself
so i started wearing white

i released it all to heal
i simplified my life
a new beginning in blank space
my canvas was pure white

i wore black in my darkness
but black was the void too
and in the void i found creation
my inspiration for the new

and in the white a purity
another way to see the void
all colors found in black and white
they led me back to joy

a bright phoenix turned to ash
but then i was reborn
so i return to color
and remember life once more

i broke my heart

somewhere along the way
i broke my own heart
and when i realized it was broken
i felt too lost to start

the path to truly healing
where do i begin?
how can i even trust myself?
how can i let love in?

what is really me?
and what is really not?
i used to be so sure of who i was
then i forgot

and so i took some time
to get to know myself
the person i once knew
got lost in someone else

i said yes when i meant no
i lived a life of "shoulds"
instead of choosing what i wanted
i didn't think i could

in those small decisions
i betrayed my inner truth
as i got older, thought i had to
i was wiser in my youth

so i took some time to feel
the confusion and the shame
the guilt and the loss
no one else to blame

it was me who broke my heart
so i could heal it too
i asked my inner child
to teach me what she knew

she taught me to have fun again
to choose what lights me up
to follow my excitement
to trust that i'm enough

so i committed to myself
to joy, to love, to truth
from there i healed my heart
and found the me that i once knew

love

why does love make us crazy?

why does love make us crazy?
why do we lose our minds?
why do we adjust ourselves?
on potential we waste time

but i guess it's not a waste
redefining time well spent
you really get to know yourself
through every message sent

with every self-betrayal
and every broken heart
you rebuild a little stronger
and see that dating is an art

an art of true expression
can we authentically relate?
a dance of different energies
to see what we create

and so it's through connection
we learn the truth about ourselves
and the craziness we feel in love
is when our ego kicks and yells

through each other we can see
where we still have open wounds
and if we're smart we'll admit
when there is energy to move

the reflections are the gift
although we might not like the mirror
and i consider time well spent
when i can see things a bit clearer

prince charming

i read a story once or twice
about a girl who fell in love
she dreamed of her prince charming
her prayers were answered from above

in each one of these stories
it works out perfectly every time
a happily ever after
we assume it all stays fine

but what about the real part?
the challenges they face?
the ups, the downs, the tears, the doubts
times they almost walk away?

they only tell us the good parts
it's just beginning when the fairy tale ends
what happens after the honeymoon?
what about kids, family, and friends?

i would love to get the whole picture
it's the truth that i want to see
because the story of that fairy-tale princess
certainly didn't happen for me

in my own way

i said no to try to save us
but it didn't work at all
it only pushed you away
i did that when i started to fall

i was afraid to love you
scared to give someone my heart
shattered so many times before
it felt safer to not even start

i ran away and i lost you
the sting of rejection too much
i secretly hoped you would chase me
but by that point you had enough

all of the games that i played
to try to keep my heart whole
only got in the way
of what i wanted deep in my soul

unshielded

there's something about the way you look at me
and the way i look at you

there's something about the way you smile
and the way your eyes pierce through

all the shields i've held up
to protect my heart inside

and all the wounds i try not to feel
are healed now that you're mine

i never thought i'd say this
but it feels good not to hide

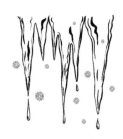

the ice queen melts

i knew after that first night
everything was going to change
you stared at me with those glittering eyes
my trepidation started to fade

i felt like ice for so long
but with you i started to melt
i had no control, and that was okay
didn't question the love that i felt

i told myself i wouldn't
but it was effortless to fall
i sank into the feeling
i had no fears at all

with you i knew i was safe
i felt your heart so pure
i knew that i could trust you
i had never been so sure

it was your love that healed me
i learned to breathe again
something i will never forget
the freest i'd ever been

comments

people made comments when we were together
about how perfect we were
people made comments when we were together
that we'd be forever, for sure

and for awhile, i thought that too
that you'd be the one by my side
but after awhile, i started to notice
an unsettled feeling inside

i tried to ignore that feeling
because it didn't make sense
you were everything i wanted
so why the dissonance?

and for a few months i battled
between my heart and my head
hoping they'd meet in the middle
but i knew that it was the end

and the hardest part about it was
i could never understand
and because of that, neither could you
it was something never planned

we were both blindsided
but you still showed up for me
you loved me even after
i said your person wasn't me

years later we reconnected
it was like no time had passed
i melted in your arms again
and wondered why it didn't last

another way

thank you for teaching me how to love
that there was another way

all i knew before was to
expect the pain and heartbreak

you saw my tender pieces
and healed them with your smile

you held me through the tears
and let me stay awhile

because of you i learned to trust
because of you i let people in

and even though you weren't my forever
with you i learned how to begin

angel

you are the one i hold onto
you are the one that i call
when i'm too afraid to open up
to anyone at all

i know i have some trust issues
but with you i don't
the betrayal i fear from others
i simply know you won't

and maybe it's because
you have some trust issues yourself
so there's a pact unspoken
that we'll protect ourselves

you're the one i lean on
when i can't stand up alone
i'm that person for everyone else
it's nice to have my own

you always make me feel
like i am welcome to lean in
and i don't hesitate
to receive the love you give

i know that you're an angel
a blessing and a gift
and i hope you know i'm always here
to lean on if you wish

love jar

wrote up all the reasons i love you
and i put them in a big jar
i told you to read one first thing each day
so you'd know my love wasn't far

it's the little things i love most about you
like the way you light up when you smile
how sometimes you're clumsy and laugh at yourself
but serious when it comes to your style

with you everything's an adventure
you romanticize things big and small
you bring me a flower whenever you see me
and every night you always call

you're obsessed with cooking new recipes
with you nothing ever goes wrong
you're always excited and for every occasion
you make a playlist and choose perfect songs

you make everybody feel welcome
you don't judge, you just hold space
you speak from your heart and somehow you always
know just the right thing to say

and there are the other small things like
your boyish grin and your tousled hair
or how whenever we drive in your car
at red lights you look over and stare

you made me an album with photos of us
and wrote a caption out for each one
you said every date was very important
that the album would never be done

i saved the love letters you wrote me
you said you sealed every note with a kiss
and whenever it seems romance is dead
i know that people like you still exist

reminders

we haven't talked for awhile
but i wanted you to know
i think of you quite often
i'll never really let you go

i genuinely wish you happiness
it brings me joy to see
how well you're doing and where you're at
i hope you wish the same for me

every day i walk by things
that remind me so much of you
a book, a sign, a card, a place
i should reach out but i never do

it feels like too much time has passed
to bother catching up
but i hope you know that doesn't mean
i don't always send you love

reciprocated

i always wanted someone
to want to truly know me
to be curious and inquisitive
and let their actions show me

they're genuinely interested
in things that make me me
that they want to understand
who i am and who i'll be

i guess i always wanted
to find someone who cares
just as much as i do
safe space for us to share

and i think it's kind of strange
when questions aren't reciprocated
are you nervous or self-centered?
more one-sided conversations

i guess i always feel like
i get them, they don't get me
to understand someone takes questions
will i find him? guess we'll see

men like to fall in love
with the way i make them feel
but they don't make me feel that way
one-sided isn't real

they love the way i make them feel
supported, understood
but i need to feel that back
with some effort, sure i could

when i really care i try to learn
the things that make you you
and i'm pretty sure that if you cared
you'd want to understand me too

not this lifetime

you say that we are soulmates
and i agree, that's true
but being soulmates doesn't mean
i'm obligated to you

i don't want to hurt your feelings
but i'm committed to being honest
you think that i'm your person
but she's not me, i promise

i want you to be happy
and i want that for me too
we might have been together before
but this time, my person's not you

can't convince me

you really didn't like it when
i said i wouldn't see you
and not just that i couldn't
but that i didn't want to

i told you it's a waste of time
when i already know
and you tried to convince me
it was a mistake for me to go

but that didn't sway me
and then you got upset
you told me you had other sides
you hadn't shown me yet

i asked you why you wanted to
convince someone to stay
instead of being with someone
who wanted you that way

with that i really hit a wound
when i pointed out the chase
the issue was self-worth
something you didn't want to face

you said because of me
you became a better man
and i'm happy for you but
don't depend upon that plan

to use me as a savior
to that i won't agree
no one else can save you
and certainly not me

you think that codependence
is how you form a bond
and that's why your relationships
often go quite wrong

the difference between us
is the way that we relate
trauma bonds, complaining
that's not the way i date

unhealthy attachment

i don't like that i hurt you
but i wouldn't take it back
because it was a byproduct
of getting my life back

it's not my job to manage
expectations or emotions
that aren't my own, and you expect
unwavering devotion

and that's fine for you to ask
but detach from who it's from
i can't give you that and i
explain i'm not the one

you're so stuck on the idea
that it has to be me
but it's not because of who i am
it's comfortability

and so when i detached
when i chose to let you go
it sort of shocked me just how much
my life returned to flow

frenemies

at first you said you hated me
not a solid start
we annoyed each other
glad to take some time apart

months later i bumped into you
a different look was in your eyes
you asked me to grab coffee
that caught me by surprise

i said yes, but went with caution
unsure of what you'd say
your demeanor was quite welcoming
it was clear something had changed

you asked me how i was
a simple lead-in to warm up
then you told me you were sorry
that the last few years were rough

you said the reason that you hated me
was something you could not explain
something in me triggered you
a truth you'd rather push away

you told me what you'd been through
how you had closed your heart
how you had acted from your wounds
and wanted a fresh start

i was honored that you trusted me
someone you hated from before
i'll admit that i had judged you
now i saw that there was more

the more you shared about your life
it became quite clear to me
i triggered you because we had
so many similarities

we had a lot more things in common
than we had seen before
from resistance to curiosity
a new relationship was born

it's funny how in one moment
everything can change
when you forgive and drop assumptions
you'll never guess what comes your way

i've learned to let go of how
i think the story ends
because someday your enemy
could become your friend

open up

you say you want something real
you say you want something deep
but i don't think you realize
you're scared of what you need

you say you feel a hole
that nothing feels quite right
you want someone who understands you
but you avoid the ones who might

you like to stay distracted
with work, parties, and women
you keep it on the surface
then complain when no love's given

if it's intimacy you crave
you'll have to open up
to let yourself be seen and heard
wanting is not enough

where that starts is with the courage
to look deeply at yourself
to love all the parts you try to hide
you're not fooling anyone else

did you know that you're quite lovable?
but you have to let her in
it's sharing what you try to hide
that lets real love begin

quality over quantity

if you had it your way
we would be much closer
but i'm stronger in my boundaries
now that i am older

you want me to relate
exactly as you do
but i'm not the type who needs more time
to express that i love you

my favorite relationships
are the ones where you just know
that nothing will ever really change
no matter how you choose to grow

quality over quantity
because talking back and forth
sometimes simply takes up space
and over time feels forced

so know if you don't hear from me
it's not that things have changed
it's not you, it's more just that
in the present i'm engaged

so i hope you can be happy
that i'm doing things for me
and talking less is not a sign
that feelings changed for me

the ultimatum

we clicked early on
it felt easy, it was fun
i never had to worry
about if you would run

you were always there for me
a solid place to lean
but i also overlooked
what else that could mean

and here i find myself again
best friend wants something more
but i'm not sure if i am ready
to open up that door

then comes the ultimatum
you want the relationship to grow
but i don't want things to change
and so i tell you no

and then i lose our friendship
and i started to regret
all the times i back away
because "more" feels like a threat

and i think about how often
i don't give things a chance
to see what it could really be
too quick to take a stance

workaholic

i made lots of money
i had lots of friends
but inside i felt empty
my life needed a cleanse

work became my lover
i wanted to succeed
no time to date—i was focused
on things i could achieve

i thought that when i "got there"
things would just work out
i pushed the goal posts further
i started having doubts

now love felt kind of scary
sounded like a lot of work
if i met someone, how could i give
the time that they deserved?

too intimidating
turned back to my career
and i pushed even harder
determination came from fear

will i end up alone?
i question what i've done
if i achieve enough,
surely i'll attract the one

suddenly it dawns on me
the love i craved to feel
i spent my whole life looking for
within my career

no amount of money
would ever be enough
and no tangible achievement
would ever fill my cup

so i made a drastic choice
i created lots of space
to manifest my person
i met him the next day

untouchable

you seem so untouchable
just out of my reach
i don't want to write you off
i wonder what you think of me

then we had a moment
i know you felt it too
like romeo and juliet
now i only think of you

you admitted you felt fireworks
but after that one night
we don't talk, you're perplexed
can't get me off your mind

we come from different worlds
but there was so much fire
i wonder how much that will
hold you back from your desire

you're trying to make sense of it
we feel so far apart
we live our lives so differently
maybe better not to start

in the silence i start wondering
am i good enough?
when secretly you pine for me
with your friends you act so tough

deep down you feel the same
are you good enough for me?
you don't want to risk rejection
am i out of your reach?

now i seem quite untouchable
we don't communicate
we both want each other but
we're stuck in a stalemate

you really start to question
if it's worth pleasing your friends
to miss the opportunity
to see how this could end

we come from different worlds
and we don't make much sense
but i can't forget someone like you
the feelings are way too intense

you still feel so untouchable
you're still the one i want
i tell myself if you reach out
i'll give this love a shot

almost six months later
i finally hear from you
you say, "who cares what they think?
i'm head over heels for you"

electricity

i don't usually get sappy
so this feels strange to say
but i have to be honest
you make me feel some type of way

every time you look at me
i melt into the floor
and with every compliment
i fall in love a little more

you're electric and magnetic
i get full body chills
every time i'm next to you
i truly can't sit still

all parts of me say yes
my body, mind, and soul
and i'll let you run away
with the piece of me you stole

i would give it all to you
if you asked for it right now
and whenever i'm with you
i see no one else around

you're always in my head
i think of nothing else
and i could try to stop it
but i can't control myself

you tell me that you feel
electricity
the times that we're together
i'm glad it's not just me

worthy

"i'll never be on your level"
"i'm not good enough for you"
you question your value in love
and it pains me that you do

i want you to know you are worthy
and there's nothing you need to do
it's simply because of who you are
and that's why i love you

you light up a room with your smile
you inspire me with your heart
i want you to know there's no need to prove
how valuable you really are

over you

you asked me if i was over you
i said i was doing just fine
from the look on your face, i know you believed me
the truth is i'm losing my mind

i don't want to admit the power
you've always had over me
i couldn't tell you that i was scared
from you i would never feel free

this was a different feeling for me
it hit my ego quite hard
i built an image of being fine on my own
believed it until i was left scarred

how could i let myself go there?
why did i let you in?
there was never really a choice
you put my head in a spin

one thing led to another
i couldn't control how i felt
you were sort of confused by me
i was a hand you hadn't been dealt

we always had a cute banter
we always kept things light
a way to stay aligned with love
we never had a fight

somehow you just got me
and i always got you too
neither of us had that before
was it too good to be true?

we left some things unspoken
we could always speak without words
but some things have to be spoken out loud
or they'll never really be heard

and so it fizzled out
as neither one jumped fully in
and i wonder if you're over me
i still get goosebumps on my skin

so no, i'm not over you
but i'll probably never tell
i assume if you really know me
you'll know i'm not doing well

unbelievable

i didn't believe in this type of connection
until you walked into my life
and as i watched it all unfold
i couldn't believe i was right

i knew that you were coming
but i wasn't ready yet
but are you ever really ready
for moments you'll never forget?

stuck in a period of disbelief
for half a year, biding my time
i didn't want to say anything
until i knew i was right

but the universe had its own plan
and it forced me to reveal
what was going on for me
and to ask you what you feel

and you listened to me patiently
as i dumped out all my thoughts
i'm just grateful you stayed open
as i explained how i connected the dots

i had no expectations
i just needed to get it out
and after i finally told you
i think i partially blacked out

after that, a heaviness lifted
finally got the weight off my chest
we agreed to let things unfold
i stopped worrying about the rest

regrets

i bumped into you in a new city
hadn't seen you in quite a while
i was surprised i felt butterflies
the second i saw you smile

a childhood crush for a decade
but we were always just friends
sometimes i thought you wanted more too
but over time "more" never happened

we moved to two different cities
and we went on with our lives
i never expected to still feel this way
not everything changes with time

we agreed the synchronicity
was a sign we should catch up
so we strolled around the local park
and decided to get lunch

you said you had your dream job
and you just got engaged
you couldn't believe where i was at now
and how much life had changed

we quickly moved past small talk
to reminiscing on old times
you said, "i had a huge crush on you"
and i said, "well, so did i"

probably shouldn't have said it
the words came out way too fast
you suddenly got quite serious
you said, "i never knew that"

i tried to laugh it off and said,
"i guess it wasn't meant to be"
you didn't laugh, you gave me a look
i'm scared what you're questioning

i changed the subject, and after the lunch
we went back on with our lives
but after that day i was stuck in my head
as i played out different timelines

the truth is i looked back with regrets
i thought about all of the times
i never said how i really felt
too nervous to cross any lines

what would have happened if we had been honest?
would life be different right now?
i realized how much of my life i suppressed
emotions pride wouldn't allow

how often do we hold back because
we're scared they won't feel the same?
instead of rejection, what if they do?
to not explore it would be quite a shame

we can't really miss what's for us
but that day i'll never forget
after that i promised to never hold back
it's not worth the chance of regret

soft spot

for you i have a soft spot
you've always known it's there
you get away with lots of things
and i don't really care

i love you but you never
hear anything you're told
we have the type of friendship
that will last until we're old

and people make remarks
about my double standards
but i don't care what they think
for you my heart is tender

you have that for me too
i know for me you soften
you always want the best for me
you tell me that quite often

it was loving, it was friendly
we got into our groove
would best friends turn to lovers?
no one really knew

and then i felt things changing
the energy had shifted
we were tied at the hip
but i noticed when you drifted

i chose to give you space
did i do something wrong?
i racked my brain for explanations
then one night you called

you told me you were sorry
nothing to apologize for
you said i hadn't done anything wrong
but that you wanted more

at first i didn't realize
exactly what you meant
was it that i'm not enough?
is our friendship at an end?

you paused and you said quietly
"that's not what i mean
the 'more' i want is with you
i can't stop these feelings"

a minute passed in silence
and you whispered my name
i decided to be honest
i told you i want the same

the drive

i'm not one to get nervous
i rarely feel self-doubt
but i'll admit that this time
i'm fully freaking out

if i'm good at anything
it's hard conversations
but this time i'm questioning
my skill of navigation

my heart is racing and
i'm struggling to breathe
i'm not even there yet
i already want to leave

my hands are shaking as i drive
the script plays in my head
i tell myself i'll be fine
i'm hanging by a thread

i wonder how you'll take it
what i'm about to say
and the second that i see you
my words all fall away

my safety blanket was my script
but i should have known
my mind would go completely blank
left there all alone

and so i paused a moment
heart racing in my chest
i found the courage to improvise
you said you were impressed

that was my reminder
no matter what life brings
i always should remember
that i can do hard things

unhinged

i've never felt so crazy
i've never felt so triggered
when i'm around you i feel out of control
and that feeling only grows bigger

i don't feel like myself
where are these emotions from?
i'm typically calm, cool, and collected
but since you i've come undone

i say i don't feel like myself
i ask myself who i've become
at the same time i'm starting to wonder
if i even knew who i was

as much as i feel out of control
as much as these feelings are new
i've also never felt more like myself
and that is because of you

who will go first?

i wonder how often you think of me
i wonder if you'll ever call
i wonder if this is all in my head
if you even feel it at all

i often think it's frightening that
we can be on such different pages
how two people in one relationship
can be at such different stages

and then i start to wonder
what's really going on?
why can't we just communicate?
is being honest really wrong?

then someone has to get vulnerable
the question is—who will go first?
give me a nudge and i'll put myself out there
if i suppress it, i think i might burst

222

2:22 on the clock
444 license plate
it's 11:11 when you pop in my head
that must be a sign that it's fate

333 is the address
on the receipt it says 5:55
there are so many signs everywhere that i look
synchronicities i can't deny

movie runtime 2:22
the main character has your last name
i open a playlist and then i press shuffle
i get a sign through the next song that plays

the book opens to page 111
and in the first sentence i find
a specific quote on priorities
last week, you said that line

it's 3:33 when you answer my text
your voice note is 2:22
there's a small chance you're playing into this but
the signs keep pointing at you

you didn't reply to my text for a week
so i yelled at the sky for a sign
you give me a call, my jaw drops in shock
because 2:22 is the time

avoidant

you say you're not avoidant
we both know that's not true
and i tell you it annoys me but
i was that way too

i tell you i don't get it
but the truth is that i do
because i used to be the one
who ran away, like you

most of my life i pretended
that i was too busy to care
the second i caught any feelings
i redirected them elsewhere

it's safer not to get in too deep
and risk breaking my fragile heart
i thought that i could stay in control
if i never let anything start

maybe push you on someone else
playing matchmaker is safe
always the one putting couples together
from my feelings i run away

or maybe suggest someone else to you
to see if you'll still choose me
my inner child still has some wounds
in feelings there isn't safety

or maybe i'll let you in,
then play an immature game
i tell you i want to be left alone
i secretly test if you'll stay

i remember that sick feeling
in self-sabotage i'm trapped
craving love with all my heart
but also too afraid of that

in self-fulfilling prophecies
i was caught for many years
from fear, i created my own pain
the cause of my own tears

in trying to protect myself
i created what i feared most
drowning in my loneliness
never let them get too close

if i was lonely either way
might as well just open up
i surrendered and to my surprise
i fell into real love

unconditional

i know you have your guard up
but i see past your walls
you can't decide if you like
that you can't hide at all

heartbroken from the past
you're not sure if it's safe
you dip your toe in, test it out
and then you back away

but unlike her, i'm patient
i'll stay firm and strong
in showing up for you because
that's where i belong

abandonment, rejection
that's what you expect
test the waters, pull away
surprised i'm not gone yet

here's what i can teach you
it's called unconditional love
it's not something you have to earn
i give it just because

vulnerability hangover
the deeper you go in
nervous system used to chaos
calmness puts you in a spin

eventually you recalibrate
deeper water feels like home
you know you're safe to swim with me
for the first time, not alone

obsessed

i cannot ever forget you
like a song stuck in my head
no matter how hard i try to move on
in my dreams you appear yet again

before you my love life was easy
then you hit me like a big truck
i've tried to go back to a love that is simple
but nobody else measures up

i know that it's not good for me
the obsession with us that i feel
i've never felt this emotion before
is this kind of love toxic, or real?

i like to think i stay grounded in love
but with you it feels way too intense
you drive me insane but i can't get enough
none of it makes any sense

sometimes i truly can't stand you
but with you i could never be mad
we go back and forth, a magnetic force
not sure if that's good or that's bad

nothing feels better than talking to you
you're my favorite person to see
we fall apart, then we come back together
and that's where i'm meant to be

my friends say you're not good for me
a bad idea from the start
but i spent so long resisting you
in the fight i broke my heart

so i surrender to the chaos
the passion and the friction
i can't wrap my brain around it but
for my heart you're an addiction

image

you tell me i'm important
that we have something special
and i was optimistic
a love so pure and gentle

but when other people got involved
i saw another side
of you i hadn't seen before
i felt the slight divide

your personality changes more
than you're willing to admit
you care most about your image
so for me that might be it

and i'm not passing judgment
i'm just saying that for me
there are things far more important
than popularity

if you're always worried
about what other people say
i can tell you now that we
will break apart some day

and so you get to choose
who you want to be
all i ask of you
is some consistency

love yourself

you want to ask for more from me
it's starting to feel forced
and i become aware of how
you use me as a source

of energy and love
and endless inspiration
i can sometimes be your muse
but not your source of motivation

your desperation tugs on me
you think that i can help
but the things you want to get from me
can't come from someone else

just one more time

you were craving love
tenderness, affection
but you wouldn't let me in
so i took it as rejection

and then you came back running
to try another time
but how am i supposed to trust
that you won't change your mind

i get whiplash from your feelings
a rollercoaster of emotions
you need to focus on your healing
before you put something in motion

and you tell me that you're ready
but i can see right through
the lies you tell yourself
your ego talks for you

shell

after him i was a shell
of the person i once was
but you pulled me out of that
you broke that shell with love

at first i didn't realize
how much i had shut down
i was used to staying silent
emotions weren't allowed

i gave you one-word answers
that wasn't good enough
you pushed me to keep talking
forced me to open up

i realized i was terrified
at how i'd be received
i thought sharing was a burden
i took on that belief

i felt my body locked
in a state of freeze
i learned expressing wasn't safe
the one who paid the price was me

and here you are, asking me
how i really feel
and what was going on for me
is your interest real?

i opened up and held my breath
how would you respond?
to my surprise, you listened
you stayed completely calm

you said you weren't surprised i felt that way
you validated me
no argument, no fixing things
for the first time i felt seen

i crawled out of my broken shell
one step at a time
you waited patiently with open arms
i hope you know that changed my life

tempestuous

your love was like the ocean
i was completely swept away
i was scared of the intensity
and so i backed away

i could've let you take me
wherever those waves might go
but i wasn't ready or willing
to go somewhere i didn't know

i didn't want to swim
i just wanted to float
you called the waves tempestuous
i relate to that the most

maybe if it was calmer
i would've given it a chance
but i think i needed my feet on the earth
to ground, to stand, to dance

two fire signs

you said "i love you" before you meant it
and i was unprepared
you said it way too early
so i left running scared

and then you called me out
for avoiding my emotions
so then i called you out
for your premature notions

you're clearly used to being
the one who calls the shots
two fire signs on battleground
and back down i will not

my sass was unexpected
you're used to getting what you want
and when it comes to me you find
it takes some extra thought

the choice

a war inside my heart
between you i must choose
he's the one who's there for me
yet i always think of you

these emotions make me crazy
i'm so caught up in my head
will i make the wrong decision?
i left you both on read

right now i feel paralyzed
my worst fear came to life
how do you choose between
what feels like day and night?

two very different kinds of loves
two different paths to take
one stable, solid, and secure
one passionate, untamed

i tell myself to focus
i know what i am worth
who brings out the best in me?
treats me how i deserve?

but when it comes to choosing love
it's not so black and white
to feel safe or to feel challenged?
deep in my heart i fight

what if both are great on paper?
what if my heart says yes to both?
in the choices with no right or wrong
we claim what we want most

in love there are no guarantees
we know we might get hurt
but i prefer the receiving end
doing it feels worse

i think about celebrating
moments big and small
when i'm excited and inspired
who's the one i call?

i think about challenges
when i'm lost and cannot see
through all the ups and all the downs
who is it next to me?

let's take it back to basics
a text pops up on my phone
whose name do i hope to see?
that's a truth i've known

there's a reason why i hope it's him
my brain can't understand
i'm sorry but my answer is
my heart had other plans

illusions

i find that people often fall
for illusions made of me
they're not ones that i create
it's what they want to see

what people seem to do with me
is create stories in their heads
then fall in love with that idea
and let the stories spread

i'm getting kind of tired of
people thinking they know *me*
when all they know is the idea
that fits with what they need

and that's why i'm so guarded
because i'm never sure about
if it's really me they love
or illusions they build out

i also start to wonder
if what they really like
is more what i can do for them
than who i am inside

they say they love the way that i
always make them feel
that's not the same as loving me
so i don't trust it's real

i'm looking for that person
who loves me just for me
who lets me show them who i am
and who i want to be

and when i meet my person
i'll know he'll really see
far beyond illusions
and appreciate what's me

be careful what you ask for

he says he wants a woman
who's independent, strong, and free
but when he finally finds her
he meets his insecurities

she'll show him where he wavers
and test how well he keeps his word
he'll realize he can't dominate
from immaturity he's cured

she will call him up
and she will call him in
captivates him with her radiance
her light will never dim

he's inspired by her boldness
impressed by her success
but deep inside it's his self-worth
he starts to second-guess

am i good enough for her?
she doesn't need me—is that bad?
without a codependent feeling
he starts to question what they have

then he realizes she stays
from desire, not from need
for the first time he feels chosen
and in love he feels free

the player

you were always confident
that you could get the girl
you know you're quite charming
but i took you for a whirl

then you realized that your charm
didn't work on me
i wanted you to open up
and really let me see

at first you liked the challenge
then you got a little scared
because what started out as fun
took you where you never dared

you didn't want to fall for me
but somehow you did
you fell hard enough to ask
if i would let you in

i didn't take you seriously
were you up to your usual games?
but in your eyes i noticed
something significant had changed

you told me that with me you saw
a future that was real
you said that with me you felt
things you were scared to feel

and all those years of chasing girls
and staying surface level
never gave you what you wanted
and you didn't want to settle

with me you're fully honest
and that's a first for you
you told me that you trust in me
i learned to trust you too

through it all, the lesson was
look where you don't expect
you had to jump when you were scared
i'm grateful that you leapt

tongue-tied

you try to tell me how you feel
but you can't find the words
because with me you know it's real
for the first time you feel heard

and i think it's kind of cute
how you get tongue-tied when we talk
your voice gets high and shaky
as you tell me what you want

and i don't make a sound
as i let you find your words
the ones you settle on are perfect
but i can feel your nerves

it's the first time you've experienced
this type of deep connection
it brings out your insecurities
you're cautious of deception

but i'm grateful that you trust
you can be vulnerable with me
a side of you you've never shared
a precious gift for me

i know that you'll stay cautious
taking one step at a time
and i remind you that you're safe
to show your heart, and i'll show mine

ice cream shop

you have a certain flavor
that might sound strange to say
but i would recognize it
anywhere and any day

and what i mean by flavor
is an energy you leave
a color, taste, and texture
it's like a drug to me

you're my favorite flavor
is that too bold to say?
i love the way it makes me feel
i hope that flavor stays

and if you were an ice cream shop
i'd stop by every day
to order that same flavor
from you i'd never stray

i wish you knew

i wish you didn't settle
i wish that you could see
what a prize you truly are
all the things that you could be

you choose the ones who treat you
like you are second best
they make you jump through hoops
and still, no approval yet

i'm not sure why you choose the ones
who never put you first
who blame you for what's not your fault
who always break their word

you're blinded by the image
you're caught up in the chase
for validation from the people
who love to only take

i wish that you could see
you deserve so much better
while you tried to please those people
you lost a love that was forever

my constant

thank you for being my constant
someone who truly cares
years, jobs, and cities change
you're the one who's always been there

thanks for being my person
you see the truth in my soul
you know me better than i know myself
with you things never get old

if we're on opposite sides of the world
i'll still feel like you're here
you're like home, you're my safe place
to share both my heart and my fears

those are the best kinds of friendships
the ones where you don't need to talk
the ones where you're safe to change and evolve
to be anyone that you want

thanks for always having my back
loyalty can be hard to find
you've always seen the best in me
and you've stood up for me every time

thanks for knowing the things i can't say
when i'm choked up and can't find the words
thanks for letting me just be myself
for holding space where i always feel heard

as time goes on and i change
so do relationships too
but as seasons change and people leave
my constant will always be you

simple love

there are times i'm lonely
and i think of times with you
the memories that never fade
the truest love i knew

the days we went exploring
those late nights in the park
breaking into places
not allowed in after dark

or the times we laughed so hard
tears streamed down my face
the nights we danced around your room
my favorite happy place

blasting music, windows down
we sang loud in the car
we never really knew the words
but we made it pretty far

i loved it when you looked at me
that glimmer in your eyes
it made me feel like you could see
the things i tried to hide

i miss when we played stupid games
up all night till dawn
and when we played with silly string
and ruined the whole lawn

i miss when you would hold me
you could heal me with a hug
helped all my worries melt away
and that's how i knew love

upside down

the second i saw you
everything shifted
my whole world
turned upside down

everything i thought
i knew for sure
no longer
had solid ground

and from that point on
i started to question
the person i wanted to be

because with you,
from your reflection,
i finally started to see

gravity

my entire body tingles
when i feel him look at me
ever since we met
i'm pulled to him like gravity

he sends shivers up my spine
the way he holds me close
and without a single word
he always knows what i need most

i get goosebumps every time
he wraps his arms around my waist
i forget to breathe, i look at him
i'm swept away

when i feel him look at me
my heart pounds so hard that it melts
i know the way he looks at me
is the deepest love i've ever felt

finding you

every time my heart broke
every tear that fell
every time i screamed and cried
secrets i would never tell

my entire body aching
shattered into pieces
unable to forget
the love, the pain, the reasons

every time i fought
every time i lost
every time i stitched my wounds
and all the time it cost

even though it hurt
the love that wasn't true
every single heartbreak
was worth it to find you

purpose

the ceiling

i think of all the nights
we laid there on the floor
dreaming, laughing, crying, thinking
always wanted more

it's almost like the ceiling
had the answers that we sought
we always asked each other
if others thought the way we thought

all those nights of thinking
as we laid there on the floor
were the nights that kept me sane
a way we could explore

that ceiling gave the answers
through the heartbreak and the grief
the things i felt that kids our age
weren't supposed to see

and then as we got older
we got some clarity
the way we thought was different and
who we were meant to be

dreamer

i got lost in my dreams
somehow swept away
and the truth is that's the place
i'd often rather stay

i know i have a habit
of getting lost up there
but down here it feels heavy
and then i'm asked to care

about things i have no interest in
it's a waste of time
to expend so much energy
creating problems in your mind

when i'm lost in my dreams
i float away in peace
and while you get caught in drama
i rise when i release

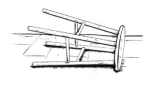

pedestal

don't put me on a pedestal
don't set me up to fall
i didn't want to be there
i don't want this at all

don't push me to be perfect
don't set me up to fail
just let me learn from my mistakes
and take my own time getting there

i'm not sure why you're so concerned
with things regarding me
focus on yourself
and who you really want to be

if you put me on a pedestal
to which i did not agree
i'll step right off—i have no interest
in comparing you and me

.

aftertaste

it left me with an aftertaste
the interaction that we had
i'm still trying to figure out
if i think it's good or bad

i know i need to trust myself
but sometimes i forget
instead i think way too hard
i get way too in my head

i've learned that first impressions
are not always what they seem
but the aftertaste will tell you
what people really mean

so i trust my intuition
even if it makes no sense
when i disregard the aftertaste
it's always something i regret

priorities

other girls around me
dreamed of the husband, house, and kids
i thought something was wrong with me
when i never really did

she's wanted it since childhood
a family, dog, and home
i wanted a top-floor penthouse
and lots of space to call my own

and people started to question
the choices i made for myself
why i liked the letters CEO
a craving that they never felt

i told them i had plenty of time
i could focus on other things later
i have to follow what lights me up now
joy is my indicator

i knew that they didn't get it
they said to get my priorities straight
i wondered why they thought mine were "wrong"
i wanted the choice to create

the life for myself that followed no rules
one where i was finally free
and when i did that, and made my own choices
i became the happiest me

the thing about priorities
is they always get to change
life moves through different phases
and our desires rearrange

i'm not saying mine are right or wrong
but i found what works for me
is trusting how i feel right now
and allowing flexibility

if you choose priorities that
are not really your own
don't be surprised if you're not happy
with your family, friends, and home

before you pass any judgment
on anyone else's life path
i invite you to ask yourself
if you're willing to do all the math

on all of the time you've spent choosing
because of somebody else
people live from a template society set
they think it means they're "doing well"

enjoy your own priorities
staying true to you
but don't expect what works for me
to also work for you

hamster wheel

i'd like to stop assuming
that it's always my fault
when people are unhappy
i take that on a lot

i wonder where that comes from
but of course i know
we're taught that we're deficient
if we don't know what we don't know

and so we get set up to feel
like we never can succeed
running on a hamster wheel
no time to rest and breathe

so i choose liberation
from responsibilities not mine
"i don't know" is what i'll own
other pressures, i'll decline

homebody

do you want to know a secret?
it's about when i'm alone
people always question why
i like to be at home

and i think it's kind of funny
how people think it's strange
i'd rather be alone than go
to fancy parties with big names

it's because i have uncovered
what i really need
to choose my own happiness
is to choose what brings me peace

and if you hate the silence
you probably can't relate
but i really like myself
and lots of open space

good questions

i feel safer asking the questions
than being on the other side
but the danger i feel over there
also makes me feel so alive

my love language is questions
it's the way i know if you care
the way i respond tells us both
if with you i'll really go there

there's something about a good question
that really opens me up
it's like finding the key to unlock the door
that you know has always been shut

so don't be afraid to ask me
what you really want to know
it's usually the question we're too scared to ask
that takes us where we want to go

settling

my deepest fear is settling
i'm strong in my self-worth
i make it very clear to you
i know what i deserve

but when emotions get involved
things aren't so crystal clear
is it settling or compromise?
i will not choose from fear

some people are afraid to lose
things they might not get back
others think the grass is greener
be careful of that trap

appreciate the things you have
that's what most of us are told
but often leaving good for great
is how miracles unfold

what if we can appreciate
but also desire more?
what if desire is intuition
saying open one more door?

so i have to go for it
i have to trust that nudge
if i'm living in "what if?"
that question is enough

enough to know there's something else
my soul wants to explore
i cannot settle for good enough
when my heart knows there is more

a lot

you said i was "a lot"
and i wonder what that means
you meant it as an insult
sounds like a compliment to me

i ponder the alternative
if it's a little or a lot
i'll always choose all of me
over something i am not

i won't apologize for bigness
or being who i am
in fact that's what i celebrate
doing all i can

and if i am "a lot"
sounds like big energy to me
if that makes you uncomfortable
then maybe less is what you seek

the vault

lots of people trust me
lots of people know
that they can spill their secrets
and in my vault they go

so i carry all those secrets
and i'm grateful that they trust
that i will keep it all inside
but sometimes i combust

because there's so much pressure
from everything i keep
i never let the secrets out
but my emotions often leak

i was looking for someone
to help relieve the pressure
someone to hold my secrets
and see them as a treasure

and more than just the pressure
i thought it would be nice
to have someone to talk to
the option for advice

and in my exploration
it finally was clear
how many people dumped on me
and then they disappeared

so i won't take your secrets
unless it's equal trade
because reciprocation
is how true friends are made

psychic

is there something wrong with me?
my emotions feel too deep
i'm trapped by sensitivity
i see things they can't see

overwhelmed with stimulation
i feel how they feel
i hear the things not said out loud
i'm not equipped to deal

used to think it was a weakness
highly sensitive, they said
too much input every day
others' thoughts are in my head

for awhile, felt imprisoned
in my body and my mind
i saw the world in layers
felt too much that wasn't mine

crippled by my empathy
there must be some way out
someone said i'm psychic
what are they talking about?

i rethought my weakness
i uncovered it was strength
i found i could read energy
a gift i'd never give away

i realized my intuition
had been loud and clear all along
i had spent so many years of my life
trying to make myself wrong

i thought something was wrong with me
just couldn't let things go
lights, smells, noises, feelings
knew things i shouldn't know

if you think you're too sensitive
there's a chance it's good information
most overlook their intuitive gifts
it's like your own radio station

anxiety and depression
haunted me for years
when i learned to use my psychic gifts
those issues disappeared

all i know is it's my gift
to see the things unseen
to know the truth unspoken
my intuition protects me

i feel things quite intensely
but i also see through lies
the answers are clear whenever i need them
intuition guides me each time

save your breath

most people wouldn't believe
the things that i have seen
the experiences that shaped me
and what has made me me

and so i keep it quiet
i wait until i'm asked
to share without invitation
feels like an unnecessary task

i decided to never be in
convincing energy
but i'm also an open book
and in that i am free

this is how i gauge who is
curious and who's not
which saves me quite a bit of time
it's curiosity i want

so some days i am quiet
and others i am loud
but that's determined by the resonance
of who might be around

silence

you'll find answers in the slow-down
when you're pushed there, it's a gift
just let yourself relax and be
it's not something to resist

i know you're scared of slowness
afraid of what you'll find
avoiding all your thoughts and
all the feelings stuck inside

but over time they'll just build up
it's time to set them free
to find the truth within yourself
that you're afraid to see

it's always in the slowness
that energy can shift
your frequency recalibrates
and then you find the gift

in all the going and the doing
you get in your own way
of experiencing the life that you've
worked so hard to make

but you're afraid of silence
you're scared to feel alone
you're afraid to face the truth
avoiding what you know

but what if in the silence
and taking some time off
you find you're not alone
and your potential is unlocked?

you're exhausted, you feel trapped
you say things need to change
but if you want to find your answers
it's yourself you'll have to face

the arena

i paced back and forth in my room
unsure who to ask for advice
my heart said to take the big leap
my brain said—don't roll the dice

i don't often ask for opinions
but i needed to hear the harsh truth
there was only one person i thought of
it obviously had to be you

i sent you a text and i asked you
am i crazy to leave what i built?
i want to quit everything, start it all over
i'm held back by the fear and the guilt

you answered me with that quote about
the arena and the man
you said i'd regret not doing the things
that both of us know i can

all i needed was that reassurance
you believed in what i could do
and the fact that you didn't hesitate
helped me believe in me too

i took a screenshot of that text
and i reread it every day
it reminds me i can't live in "what if"
that this life is my game to play

you gave me the courage to go for it
you said not to limit my dreams
that greatness was something not everyone chooses
but that you could see it in me

and everyone else had opinions
you taught me to shut out the noise
to hold the big vision and let them all see
the power of just one brave choice

shine bright

i kept it quiet—my success
because i knew that you
would feel intimidated, maybe jealous
tear down what i grew

i learned to make myself small
so you would feel okay
but when i chose your comfort
i gave my confidence away

it's not real love, it's not support
if it's based on your conditions
it's not on me if you're triggered by
accomplishment and ambition

so i've learned to not apologize
for taking space and shining bright
the truth is that to change the world
we cannot dim our light

i've decided to be proud of
who i am and what i've built
they push us to do more, but when we do
we're pushed to guilt

don't be too much, don't shine too bright
don't take up too much space
but don't be lazy, don't play small
what more can you create?

don't be afraid to outgrow people
and shift the paradigms known
if someone's afraid of your power
the relationship could never grow

i decided to shine a bright light instead
of dimming who i really am
and if me staying small makes you feel secure
then on shaky ground we stand

i don't have space for jealousy,
competition, or anything fake
but what i will do is own what's my truth
and share all the magic i make

breaking open

you push me to surrender
you tell me to let go
of all the fear, the strength, the walls
to let emotions flow

but i'm afraid to break
what if the tears don't stop?
i don't want you to think
i am someone i am not

i am used to my emotions
being used against me
but if they were safe to flow
i know that i'd feel free

i refuse to let the people
who hurt me in the past
block me from my power
effects not meant to last

so i open to surrender
and i let you see me raw
the dam broke open, and as it flowed
it was beauty that you saw

surprise

i've learned that when i overplan
things always go awry
so i'm leaning into living life
in the energy of surprise

we try to plan for safety
but does it really work out?
the best things in my life have been the things
i had no idea about

living in the unexpected
requires a level of trust
but if i want a life of miracles
releasing control i must

if i overthink it
i know that i'll back out
fully living in the present
i forget to have my doubts

so i let myself stay curious
i'm always open to the new
the greatest gifts in life aren't planned
i mean, that's how i met you

flow

i find myself addicted
to deep connection with myself
emotions, creativity
a flow like nothing else

people stay busy looking for
that feeling somewhere outside
in the search for a connection
they also often hide

they hide from their own feelings
they hide from inner truths
and in the process block themselves
from being their own muse

i wonder what would happen
if you spent more time alone
maybe you'd surprise yourself
in yourself you might find home

resistance

you say that i'm not trying
but i question why i should
you think that it should take hard work
if it was easy, no one would

when it comes to working hard
at some point we must look
at the compatibility
of what we want to work

if you're overly committed
to your way working out
you might miss opportunities
that are better, but you doubt

i understand commitment
but i also know
that when it's truly for me
it will feel like ease and flow

kind of weird

you think i'm kind of weird
but you kind of like it, too
because the things that are weird about me
also remind you of you

so let's be weird together
it's easier that way
with me you can just be yourself
let go of the roles that you play

but the thing that truly scares you
is letting all of you be seen
what a shame to hide who you are
and let your ego intervene

all of the things you want
will come in when you just relax
the things that make you unique
are the power that you have

you want to create something different
yet you make choices so you fit in
but your weirdness is your real magic
my door is open—let yourself in

iconic

she lived to be iconic
she lived to set the tone
she had aspirations to be
someone quite well-known

she got everything she wanted
in the process got caught up
the deeper she got in
felt nothing was enough

she didn't understand
what came with what she wished
didn't know what she does now
her life before was what she missed

she felt trapped in what she wanted
didn't know the cost of fame
the judgment, the projections
when they all knew her name

with everyone around her
she still always felt alone
the parties and the traveling
she missed a sense of home

i knew her from the magazines
and then one day we met
the more i got to know her
i could tell she had regrets

the thing is, she's just human
and she told me it was nice
to pretend she wasn't famous
felt like a normal life

we might have big dreams
of what our perfect lives would be
but what if when we get there
we still do not feel free?

lonely

i know that you feel lonely
for a long time i did too
and here's the secret that i found
i had to embrace the new

i chose new experiences
and new ways of relating
embraced new people in my life
new styles of communicating

i had to form new habits
i had to open up
i had to share who i really was
facades were not enough

but that required me
to be honest with myself
and in that process i realized
i had betrayed myself

i was keeping myself stuck
by not owning who i was
i was hiding from my truth
kept choosing fear instead of love

so i started to explore
who i really am
and it was the authentic me
i decided i would share

i had to be okay with who
would stay and who would go
i had to learn to be okay
with releasing what i'd known

intimidating

you say i'm intimidating
because i'm firm in my beliefs
am i intimidating?
or are you intimidated by me?

you find it unsettling
that not much shakes me up
that anytime you go too far
i will tell you that's enough

you don't really like it
that i will call you out
it scares you when i disagree
and when i voice my doubts

you call me intimidating
because of my ambition
because i never wait around
to bring desires to fruition

you think it's intimidating
because real confidence is rare
you like to be passive aggressive
you're triggered that i don't care

you say i'm intimidating
like it's an attribute
instead of recognizing it's
a response from within you

do you realize when you call me that
it says more about you?
if you're really that intimidated
it reflects a deeper truth

when you're truly confident
there are other words you choose
like interesting or inspiring
your ego not left bruised

if what it is is jealousy
then i'll give you a clue
if it's possible for me then
it's also possible for you

simplify

i felt like i should simplify
the clutter in my life
i felt like it became too much
trapped by internal strife

and so i started to release
the things i did not need
as i let go of attachments
it felt easier to breathe

weight lifted off my shoulders
one by one i let go
and with that extra space
there was room for me to grow

but with every cord i cut
i felt guilt, shame, and doubt
what will they all think of me?
what judgments will they cast out?

i realized i collected
lots of things to take up space
to avoid sitting in silence
and truths i didn't want to face

about who was really there for me
and who, in fact, was not
about what was giving me energy
and what was taking a lot

i didn't want to admit how much
i needed to let go
didn't want to release the clutter
with it, i felt less alone

i realized i added more things
to avoid the emptiness inside
i thought the busier i was
i'd feel a little more alive

but the more things i added
i grew resentful and confused
it wasn't my job to hold onto things
that left me feeling used

and so i learned my lesson
be careful what you keep
the cost of undoing things
will teach you what you really need

it's not more money, friends, or time
there's a price to saying yes
i learned i had to say more "no's"
to circumvent a bigger mess

what i really needed
was just some extra space
to learn to love myself again
and give myself some grace

drama queen

you say that i'm dramatic
and maybe that is true
but it takes one to know one
and you like drama too

i'm anything but boring
isn't that a plus?
that's why you were drawn to me
that's why you wanted us

and you call it dramatic
when i express my feelings
at first i didn't care but now
i think that needs some healing

if you're scared of my emotions
that's on you, not me
in what you call chaotic
i find my alchemy

i used to hate emotions
they used to scare me too
i never knew what to expect
but over time i grew

i had the realization that
that was the whole point
feelings gave me liberation
they're how i found my voice

people fear emotions
"please don't make a scene"
but when i learned how to express myself
i finally felt free

conditional

he only loves me when i'm happy
she only loves me when i'm sad
he hates when i get frustrated
wants to fix all these feelings i have

she doesn't like when things are going too well
because she feels like it's a threat
she can't relate unless i'm complaining
she's more comfortable when i'm upset

when i detoxed my life i finally saw
the dysfunction in how we relate
in romance it's only safe if you're fine
in friendships you bond over hate

so i dropped relationships limiting me
from feeling emotions i have
i focused on people who love and forgive
not the ones who choose to stay mad

i focused on people who celebrate life
and bond over joy and big dreams
that pissed off the people who like to stay stuck
being around that only trapped me

if it's only through problems you like to relate
then that's how you'll keep finding more
and if fake positivity is all you can handle
then our depths we can never explore

relationships keep people stuck
i know it's a tough pill to swallow
who we love isn't always healthy for us
underneath the connection feels hollow

i chose happiness when i decided
what i was truly available for
authentic feelings, just being myself
anything less, you'll always crave more

simple, but complex

life is complicated
things aren't just black and white
sometimes people fall in love
in the middle of a fight

sometimes life seems simple
other times it seems complex
i have two opposing thoughts
at once inside my head

emotions tug us both ways
we crave the things we hate
addicted to our vices
hard to walk away from pain

say one thing, and do another
what do we really think?
i think most of us don't really
know what we believe

we say we want it one way
then we choose something else
i think i'm getting whiplash
from emotions that i felt

we say we want companionship
won't open up our hearts
we want love, but it might hurt
so safer not to start

we say we want to be happy
but we won't allow ourselves
the things that we desire
compromise for something else

we have lots of dreams
but we're not sure what to do
what if it doesn't work?
smarter not to make a move

walking contradictions
and then we wonder why
we're confused and unfulfilled
cognitive dissonance applied

people aren't just good or bad
we have shadows with our light
choices aren't just pros and cons
that's the complexity of life

analysis paralysis
back in forth inside our heads
i've decided for my sanity
to let my heart lead me instead

open book

i know you think it's personal
but i'm an open book
i explore the places
others wouldn't dare to look

so you can ask me anything
in fact, i want you to
i like when i get pushed to
answer questions that are new

that is how i learn the truth
of who i really am
that's how i continue to
evolve in ways i can

i'm not afraid to explore
the places that are dark
and if you guide me there
on me you'll truly leave your mark

i see that as the greatest gift
finding someone who's the type
to lead with curiosity
instead of being right

so no, don't be afraid
to push me to my edge
because it's to expansion
i've made a lifelong pledge

you can join the fun with me
if you want to try it too
you might just find facing your fears
unlocks the magic within you

uncaged

living from my ego
is how i trapped myself
i felt imprisoned in my life
from my cage i wanted out

that was my own doing
something i created in my mind
let my wounds make my decisions
felt i was running out of time

we make choices based on stories
illusions that aren't true
where is it that those come from?
programs we get to undo

living from my heart
was an ego hit for sure
but there is instant freedom
in intentions that are pure

love, compassion, soul desire
now guide all i do
if i could create my own cage
i can create my freedom too

timelines

what would life be like
if you knew what's coming next?
people think they want to know
be careful what you manifest

they think that if they knew for sure
that then they could calm down
assurance it will be okay
that it will all work out

but do you really want to know
what the end result will be?
don't forget that you create
your own reality

what if you knew ahead of time
what you didn't want to know?
what if it's your destiny
to go where you don't want to go?

would you still say yes to people
you knew were short-term friends?
would you still go into it
if you knew there'd be an end?

would you say yes to love right now
if it wasn't for forever?
would you choose the best in front of you
if down the road you know there's better?

you think you want to know the plan
to make the right decision
but don't forget you can create
the life that you envisioned

your mind might think there's right and wrong
but they're just different paths
so take responsibility
for the power that you have

interwoven with those paths
you'll find destiny
but depending on how you choose
she'll show up differently

if you knew ahead of time
your ego might say no
to the lessons truly meant for you
that let your highest path unfold

to know the timeline in advance
you'd have to learn to be okay
with saying yes to things you knew
would fall apart some day

can you trust yourself enough to choose
what might cause you pain
if it aligns you with the path
where you have everything to gain?

your soul sees the big picture
but the ego likes control
maybe it's better to live in the present
trust you know what you need to know

unapologetic

she's a free and wild spirit
lives life from intuition
unapologetically herself
she has no inhibitions

she makes some people nervous
don't know what to expect
they're scared of unpredictable
and what she might do next

it frustrates many people
she cannot be controlled
unwavering in confidence
strong opinions, actions bold

it says a lot about the people
who fret she can't be tamed
while others are inspired
and respect her for the same

some people call her selfish
others call her brave
either way, she doesn't care
it's only freedom that she craves

searching

i was always searching
always looking for the next
and everywhere i go i think,
i haven't found it yet

sometimes i move so fast
i don't have time to feel
i don't take time to stop and think
and celebrate what's real

living in the future
i don't think i'll catch up
and living in the past is like
nothing's good enough

i can live in the nostalgia
or potential that could be
but in the chase i miss the truth
of my reality

i wonder what it is that stops me
from living in the now
what i'm scared to feel and know
what will the space allow?

i looked so far ahead
got overly attached
stuck living in potential
that's time i won't get back

my ego took a hit
when i allowed myself to see
that everything i want and need
is right in front of me

so i committed to myself
and i committed to my now
i detached from what "should be" delivered
and i detached from knowing how

and in the letting go i found
my soul could guide the way
to what was truly meant for me
and happiness that stayed

saturday donuts

when i was five you held me close
checked for monsters in my room
when i cried myself to sleep at night
you'd lie there with me too

my safe place was a fantasy book
pretended i could read
we spent hours in the bookstore
that was my favorite treat

so were saturday donuts
the sprinkled pink ones were the best
you'd go pick some up for me
while i watched cartoons in your king bed

when i was eight you showed me
my creativity
to dance and write short stories
to dream of who i'd be

you bought me an electric piano
played for hours in the car
wasn't good, so switched to dance
no practice was too far

i thought i might try softball
never used that brand-new glove
instead i played with makeup
tried red lipstick—it was love

i always felt a little different
by thirteen i was stressed
stayed distracted from the things i felt
with homework, sports, and friends

by seventeen you saw me
cry far too many times
i was cracking under pressure
i pretended i was fine

i was sitting on my bed
staring at the wall
you sat down right next to me
the silence said it all

you told me to slack off a bit
you wished that i could see
that if i wasn't perfect
you'd still be proud of me

you told me i could be a kid
i grew up way too fast
to spend more time on teenage things
high school wouldn't last

i didn't really know why
i carried so much on my shoulders
you wished that you could take the weight
i could worry when i'm older

by nineteen things got heavier
of my health i lost control
you wished that you could save me
on us all it took a toll

i felt hopeless, you were scared
so we took it day by day
we went on weekend getaways
to take my mind off of the pain

by twenty-two i took off running
couldn't keep up with my plans
out of darkness, no time wasted
shocked at just how fast i ran

that's the thing you taught me—
that i could handle speed
and no matter what might come my way
in my dreams i could believe

so i built the life i wanted
unconventional—that's me
and you learned about my weird new fads
with each identity

and now at twenty-seven
i don't think that you know
my entire life is built upon
something you told me once at home

i was feeling broken, lost
and scared to take a leap
you hugged me while i cried and what
you shared next shifted me

you said every time you've leapt
you weren't ready or prepared
you took risks that made no sense
you jumped when you were scared

but that you always found
somehow it just worked out
when you know what makes you happy
follow that, release the doubt

you told me not to worry about
how things fall into place
that the universe was on my side
and from my heart to never stray

now i live life based on that trust
that lesson truly changed my world
and know that even as years pass
i'll always be your little girl

no coincidences

do you ever stop and think about
how the most important person in your life
might not be the most important,
or even present, over time?

i look around and think about
how my reality
right now looks like nothing i
expected it would be

my most important people now
i didn't even know last year
what if next year's people
haven't even entered my sphere?

i also often think about
if i pop in random people's heads
i might not even know them
maybe they're next year's friends

it's never a coincidence
when someone pops into your head
don't dismiss it, it's not random
people play it off instead

we're always getting messages
about what's been and what could be
nothing is coincidence
it's called telepathy

do you realize you're connected
to your future, present, and past?
when you get those not-so-random thoughts
don't move on quite so fast

letting in new people and
letting relationships change
doesn't mean they're less significant
just time for things to rearrange

if you're in the flow of life
where change is how things go
it's only natural to encounter
new things you don't yet know

you might be afraid of change
but if you hold on way too tight
you might miss opportunities
to meet the best people in your life

writing the rules

people think i'm crazy
i build then tear it down
but i can't stick with just one thing
in boredom i would drown

i decide to feel unlimited
from there all good things flow
where my inspiration takes me
i will gladly go

the trick has always been
do not overthink it
if i do, i'll back out
i'll always find good reasons

if my logic and my heart
are not on the same page
i always trust my soul because
logic plays a game

the game of what can work
the game of what makes sense
but i don't want a life where i
settle for content

what it really takes to build
an extraordinary life
are lots of leaps of faith
trusting your soul over your mind

and so, will you do it?
i ask, who will you be?
will you choose to play it safe
or will you choose to take the leap?

will you choose to stay limited
by what's been done before?
or will you choose a life
of creating something more?

the one thing that i ask myself
with each decision that i make
is what choice i want to stand by
which path i'm proud to take

and with every single choice
we show who we are
we show if we choose fear
or if we choose to set the bar

i choose to push the limits
not just do what's been done
life's a game, i write the rules
in doing so, i've won

confidence

they ask me how i'm confident
have i always been that way?
the truth is that i haven't been
it was a choice i made one day

if i identified with "insecure"
then that was who i'd be
so i decided to be confident
and show up differently

when i chose my confidence
i saw myself through a new lens
i realized my first step was to
become my own best friend

the first way i built confidence
was keeping promises to myself
i realized all the times
i compromised my needs for someone else

the next way i built confidence
was deciding i would listen
to the inner voice guiding me
to trust my intuition

and from there i recognized
how often i looked to someone else
for advice or for approval
trusting them over myself

all the times i broke my promises
the ones i made to me
were times of self-betrayal
something before i couldn't see

how could i ever trust myself
if i had never kept my word?
how i really built my confidence
was making sure that i felt heard

for a long time i hoped someone would
prove i could count on them
but the person who i needed most
was me, my own best friend

when i anchored in my confidence
was when i showed up for myself
in heavy times, at my lowest points
i turned to me for help

i learned that i could count on me
from then on i was home
safe space always found within
even when i was alone

do you know what makes you confident?
owning who you are
being yourself without apology
being proud of every scar

do you know what makes you confident?
learning every part of you
diving deep in every corner
loving the light and shadow too

and now that i have confidence
i've learned to be okay
with projections and assumptions
the judgments thrown my way

the same people who want confidence
are the ones who like to say
that confidence is arrogance
in insecurity they stay

let's not confuse humility
with making yourself small
to be humble requires confidence
to truly see the love in all

so with confidence i trust my myself
to be all that i can be
and if i bet on anyone
it will always be me

pattern interrupt

some say that people never change
and some say that they do
personally i think they can
but most people don't choose to

that's the thing—it's a choice
a conscious redirection
and there's often some discomfort
we stay the same for false protection

and people say it's hard
to repattern what they do
i guess it is if you decide
that habits control you

or you can decide
to make the change is easy
because you're the one in control
of things you keep believing

purpose

an existential crisis
what's the reason that we're here?
disconnected from my purpose
the reason wasn't clear

i can't believe that work, routine,
and small talk could be it
if every day just feels the same
to that i can't commit

i always felt a craving
there must be something more
so i became obsessed with
exploring every door

over time i told myself
it might just take some time
but the deeper i got into it
i thought i lost my mind

i started to follow my passions
and something shifted in me
but as much as they filled my cup
in my life i didn't feel free

i felt close in loving friendships
in romance even more
in living my gifts i felt purpose
i could fly, but i wanted to soar

why did i feel something missing?
i was tortured by what it could be
it had to be love, and one day i realized
the love i wanted was always in me

leaps of faith

i've learned that playing safe
never gets me what i want
so i take the leap of faith
and it works out quite a lot

people want big things
but they let their fear decide
and if you live that way
do you really feel alive?

i find the big decisions
the ones that shake you in your boots
are the most expansive
and build the strongest roots

what i mean by that is
in always choosing trust
you build a strong foundation
because nothing shakes you up

how can you be confident
in taking leaps of faith?
i know that i'll always be caught
it happens every day

and what you might perceive
as putting trust in something else
is actually what i perceive
as fully trusting in myself

radiant

i always wanted to be like her
confidence, success, and heart
she radiated joy and love
and effortlessly stood apart

she followed her intuition
did things they never could
she made it look so easy
to live the life she said she would

i visualized her nightly
getting familiar with the feeling
of abundance, ease, and grace
and then i focused on my healing

i spent so long focused inward
i forgot that childhood dream
until one day i realized
that woman was actually me

her

there are moments i tune in
to the beating of my heart
when i'm scared, i tell myself
i only need to start

when there are times i think
there is no way forward
i remember with that thought
i am choosing my own torture

so what would it feel like
to create my happiness?
i tune into my heart and she
reminds me of this—

i can choose to fall
or i can choose to rise
i can choose to get back up
or i can choose to hide

and all the strength i need
i find within my heart
she is power, she is wisdom
from her i never part

mothers

thank you to my mothers
the ones who hold me close
who see my heart and wipe my tears
somehow they just know

i find mothers all around
it's in a heartfelt hug
it's when you squeeze me tight and
check up on me just because

it's when you see into my soul
it's when you hold some space
it's when you say to keep on crying
instead of saying it's okay

it's in moments when she comforts me
and i feel truly heard
it's how she just knows what i need
when i haven't said a word

she's the one who sees my magic
the one who knows what's really me
who sees my pure intentions
and from love she always sees

i find her in my friendships
the ones where i am safe
i let my guard down and she meets me
with a warm embrace

i feel her in nature
the big oak tree i found
the fresh green grass, the cold soft dirt
there are mothers all around

divine

when you feel alone and
like no one's on your side
remember who you are
in essence you're divine

when you forget your purpose
when you're not sure what to do
remember when you follow joy
the divine will work through you

i hope you know you're not alone
i hope you know that there's a reason
we need your magic in the world
it's something to believe in

in being yourself, you share a gift
that's all you have to do
live from love—that's your mission
the universe guides you

surrender

"how do i let go?" she asked
"how do i surrender?"
it's not something you learn to do
it's something you remember

it's like asking how to learn
to blink your pretty eyes
or how to breathe or how to fall
asleep when it's nighttime

it's actually more natural
than forcing your way through
i know that we are taught to force
but letting go works too

because you'll find when you hold on
to things that shouldn't be
you get tired and feel the weight
of stagnant energy

so if you want your life to move
turn down the extra noise
release the things not serving you
surrender is a choice

disruptors

sometimes they say to slow down
sometimes they say to speed up
for me, i like to pump the brakes
when i want to shake things up

there's something about disruption
that shakes them to their core
for me that's how i stay engaged
i open brand-new doors

i think it's kind of funny how
people really like to complain
they want it to be different
but they'll never instigate a change

so here's to all the changemakers
the ones who break the rules
the ones who follow intuition
over what they learned in school

if you really want a change
it all begins with you
you can choose your happiness
if you stop hiding from your truth

synchronicities

the universe is speaking
but you have to want to hear
otherwise you'll miss it
the signs are always near

the universe is showing you
exactly where to go
but you have to want to see the truth
you have to want to know

and once you start to listen
once you choose to see
you might become overwhelmed
with all the synchronicities

and from there you recognize
the places you were blind
you thought that there was nothing there
the key an open mind

and then you start to realize
there were answers all along
all you had to do was ask
and stop being so headstrong

the universe will speak to you
through people, songs, and books
through feelings and a knowing
signs are everywhere you look

so when you feel confused
and when you feel alone
get quiet, ask for guidance
and you'll find your way home

pain, love, & purpose

it's the pain that leads the way
to the wisdom deep inside
it cracks your heart wide open
gives you nowhere else to hide

and from that depth of feeling
we remember our own hearts
when we're on the path to love
sometimes pain is where it starts

the harder you might fall
the higher you can rise
from the darkness of the pain
your soul will always guide

from my pain i found my purpose
my feelings showed my truth
pain guided me to passion
and what i was meant to do

when i avoided feeling pain
i blocked myself from love
through pain, love, & purpose
i found who i really was

it's the pain that brings us to our knees
and teaches us surrender
and from that open-hearted place
it's love we can remember

it's often through the pain
illusions come undone
from there the truth can rise
our purpose here is love

thank you

in your hands right now
you hold my heart
thank you for keeping it safe

in reading this book
you've seen my heart
i hope it helped you in some little way

about the author

christina rice is a writer, speaker, intuitive channel, and energy healer. her mission is to support individuals in stepping into their power and living their most authentic, abundant, and aligned lives. christina has helped thousands of people create their dream realities and master the energetics of their relationships, businesses, and health through her transformational online programs, books, and podcast–christina the channel. to learn more, visit christinathechannel.com.

Made in the USA
Middletown, DE
11 November 2022

14695148R00186